Colors of the
Spirit

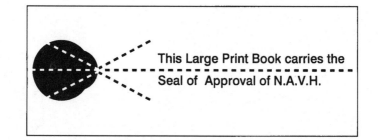

This Large Print Book carries the
Seal of Approval of N.A.V.H.

Colors of the Spirit

Dorothy K. Ederer

G.K. Hall & Co. • Thorndike, Maine

Published in 1999 by arrangement with Doubleday,
a division of Random House, Inc.

G.K. Hall Large Print Inspirational Series.

The text of this Large Print edition is unabridged.
Other aspects of the book may vary from the original edition.

Set in 16 pt. Plantin by Al Chase.

Printed in the United States on permanent paper.

Library of Congress Cataloging in Publication Data
Ederer, Dorothy K.
    Colors of the spirit / Dorothy K. Ederer.
      p.   cm.
    ISBN 0-7838-8514-8 (lg. print : hc. : alk. paper)
    1. Christian life — Catholic authors. 2. Large type books.
  I. Title.
  [BX2350.2.E334 1999]
  248.4—dc21   98-51856

I dedicate this book to my parents,
Ann and Bernard Ederer,
who have also been my best friends.
I dedicate this book as well to my brothers,
Bernard and Father John,
and to my sisters,
Carol, Jeanne, Julie, and Geralyn.
Their loyalty and support have been
unwavering through
happy and difficult times.

Acknowledgments

I could not have survived this manuscript without the patient guidance and whimsical suggestions of Joseph Girzone. His playful humor was always well timed. He has shown himself a true friend.

I want also to thank especially Pierrette Virkler, our secretary. She has been, in her quiet, dedicated way, an inestimable support.

I am grateful in a special way to Peter Ginsberg, my agent, whose faith at times seemed beyond reason, but whose encouragement has proven that we rise to the level of loved ones' expectations.

Trace Murphy, my editor at Doubleday, has become a warm friend as well as a kind and gentle critic. My gratitude to Trace is deep and lasting.

Contents

Foreword

The longer I live, the simpler life appears. What is so difficult to understand is why human beings live in such unending conflict, and continually generate so many unresolvable problems. Of late, it dawned on me what appears to be the basis for the phenomenon: No two people see things in exactly the same way. To the simple question "How are you?" one person will respond with a grateful smile and a "Fine, thank you." "Why do you ask?" will be another person's response. A simple look of bewilderment will be a third person's reaction. "It's a nice day," a fourth will reply without answering the question. "Why do you ask? Don't I look well?" another might say. Some reactions can be downright hostile. Each person's response expresses the way he or she views the question, and his or her mood at the time. The same diversity of observations is seen when a number of people have witnessed the same event. You wonder if they all saw the same thing. It is almost as if each person has a different pair of glasses which focuses on different facets of the same object and biases the viewer. And then there's human nature. Some people are happy, some are melancholy. Others are suspicious and some absolutely paranoid. I have friends who always see the dark side. One day I gave a gold piece as a present to one of these friends. His first comment was "Oh, but what am I going to do with it? I'm sure I will lose it." So the next day he sold it. I was a little annoyed, because I had been saving it for years as part of an investment for my retirement. During the next two weeks the value of that gold piece went up forty dollars. I know it was only money, but the incident taught me a lesson about the different ways people perceive things.

My father was the type of person who seemed to have been born with a happy spirit and always saw things through rose-colored glasses. Even on dismal, rainy days he would remark, "What a beautiful day!" It used to annoy me, because if it was raining, I could not see anything good about it, especially if there was no school. But he did not make such remarks just to be contrary. He really felt it was a good day. Even during the most difficult times in his life he had that same attitude. For example, he and my mother had had nine children and he was drafted into the army. The news reporters came to the house and, after asking him how he felt about being drafted, asked him what would happen to his wife and the children if he should die. His answer was a shock. "If God can use *me* to take care of the family, He can do just as good a job without me."

I think people who enter the news industry have all been born with black glasses. They seem to have an obsession with the dark and sick side of life. I hardly read the newspapers anymore; they are too depressing. I think they are responsible for the depression and hopelessness so many people feel today. Just as a family would be torn apart if one member is depressed, the worldwide family is affected by the media's emphasis on the darker side of life.

Four years ago I met Sister Dorothy. I was immediately impressed with her extraordinarily happy spirit. Her rose-colored glasses were obvious. I do not think I ever met a person who found such simple, childlike joy in life. She reminded me of Whoopi Goldberg in *Sister Act*, and Maria in the *The Sound of Music* combined. In reading *Colors of the Spirit*, I felt Dorothy's happy spirit on every page. Her love of people and her ability to see good in people where others might see only evil is so healthy and uplifting, it was truly a joy for me to read this wonderful manuscript. I think our world needs that spirit if we are ever to rekindle a sense of joy and humor in the human family. We need the hope that that outlook can inspire. One grows weary of those who are offered a pile of diamonds and look for the speck of dirt that they seem to value more than the diamonds. In *Colors of the Spirit*, Dorothy Ederer looks across a worn-out humanity and finds priceless treasures. I hope that this literary endeavor is just the beginning of her writing career. The world needs her optimism and happy, childlike spirit. It is like a songbird's return at the end of a long, cold winter. I have no doubt that this little book will quietly find its way into the hearts of the many people who are looking for bright sunshine and spring flowers.

— JOSEPH F. GIRZONE

Introduction

It doesn't matter if I pick up the newspaper, turn on the television, or listen to the radio, I am bombarded with stories about the dark side of people's lives. It seems that everything that happens throughout the world is based on endless conflict. Either it is the "crime of the century," a celebrity marriage falling apart, or the hatred that has divided people along ethnic lines in some distant (or not so distant) part of the world. Faced with all this, I can't help wondering whether the world is a sick place.

And yet I have never lost my faith in people. I have always believed that people were basically good, that in time everyone's good side would show. Maybe it is because I see people at their best so much that I found a reason for hope even in the darkest situations.

In the following pages I share with you real-life adventures. Some are my own, some are from the lives of people I have known over the years. I have been deeply touched by each of these incidents. You will see in these stories remarkable individuals who discovered the potential goodness lying

15

within and also the striking effect their lives have had on others.

Merely witnessing these powerful experiences enriched my life. They have brightened the colors of my world, a world that is sometimes darkened by the pain and desperation I often encounter in those I meet. These individuals have been a sort of spiritual rainbow, each reflecting a different color with a unique meaning. For this reason I have chosen the rainbow as the vehicle for sharing these experiences, with each color having a certain meaning. Each color I have chosen brings to mind memories and feelings associated with events that have had a powerful effect on my life. As white light is filtered through the raindrops to create a rainbow, so, too, is God's goodness and holiness filtered through all creation, manifesting itself in each of God's creatures.

God created a universe of color that profoundly affects not only our senses but our emotional, intellectual, and psychological lives. Color even influences our decision-making process. Consider, for example, how we feel when the sky is a gray. Depressed and dreary? Some people cannot live in somber areas and move to where there is more light and color. A light blue sky can brighten our whole day.

Consider also the varied shades of green that burst forth in nature in the springtime in which God has placed us. Think of how it feels walking through a cool, lush, green forest. Compare that with how it would feel to walk through the same forest with all the foliage dark brown or purple. Soft, soothing green certainly does make a difference.

The very way in which God has engineered our physical and emotional makeup renders us dependent upon color. Color enhances the food and drinks we enjoy; black champagne just would not taste the same. A glass of cold brown water does not sound very tempting, even on a hot summer afternoon. We choose our clothes according to color. We paint and design our homes with color being the number-one consideration. We even have books written about our personalities according to color. Millions of dollars are spent each year by market researchers calculating which colors attract consumers and which ones turn them off.

Colors also have metaphorical meanings. White is often used as a symbol of purity, gold as a purifying light, red as passion, purple or violet as a symbol of sin or sorrow for sin, and blue as soothing, comforting, liberating.

As you can see, I think about color a fair

amount — and I think about rainbows even more. Rainbows have always been exciting to me, but they became even more significant a few years after my dad's death. Let me tell you the story.

I was off from work on the day that would have been my dad's sixty-eighth birthday, and I decided to visit my mom. It was a three-hour drive to her mom's house. Driving along the lonely highway, I became lost in thought. I became almost hypnotized as I listened to the patter of raindrops on the windshield. Memories of my dad kept flooding my mind, as if he were trying to speak to me. I missed him and wanted to reach out to him. I began talking with my dad and shared with him all that was happening in my life. I wondered if he was pleased with me and proud of what I was doing.

Unfortunately, I started to feel frustrated with this very one-sided conversation. My dad was not responding at all, but I still felt a powerful need to converse with him, not just to talk *to* him. I wanted so much to know how he felt about my life and the work I was doing. I decided to put him on the spot and ask him to give me a sign, to let me know if he was happy with me and proud of my work. I don't know what I expected, maybe a thunderclap, or a voice. But I waited . . . expectantly. It was only minutes later that a brilliant rainbow suddenly appeared in the sky. At first I was thrilled — this was a pretty good sign! But then I started to doubt because, after all, rainbows are really not that uncommon. Why should this one be any different? I decided to up the ante. "Dad, if that is really you, give me a double rainbow!" Almost immediately a second rainbow appeared, just as bright and clear as the first. I started to cry. I knew he was with me.

As I gazed on this scene with wonderment, it occurred to me that the sun is always at the center of the rainbow — no matter what angle or perspective you see it from. The way I looked at it, I saw the sun as God, so I knew my dad was with God and they were being playful together. The two of them were there by my side. I was excited and overjoyed. I felt my dad's embrace as I never felt it before.

I could hardly wait to tell my mom. When I arrived home, I ran into the kitchen and hugged her. Surprised, she asked me, "Dorothy, what happened? Why are you so excited? Are you all right?"

"Mom, the most beautiful thing just happened to me," I told her. As I related the story, she began to cry. We both were quite emotional. "It was so beautiful, Mom. I only wish I had a camera."

That powerful moment became a treasured memory for both of us.

A few days later, after I had arrived back at work in Kalamazoo, I bumped into a parishioner coming into the church. Completely out of the blue he asked in an excited voice, "Dort, did you see that beautiful rainbow the other day?"

"Yes, I sure did. I only wish I could have taken a picture of it."

"Well, guess what, Dort? I did take a picture of it."

"You did? Can I have a copy? I would love to give it to my mom for her birthday next month."

Two weeks later he dropped the photo off at the church.

My next visit home was on my mother's birthday. I presented her with a surprise, the framed picture of the rainbow. I will never forget the surprised look of delight when she opened the package. There were tears and smiles, and she could not speak. It was as if she had seen the face of my dad smiling on her.

Many years later, when she went into a nursing home, she kept that picture by her bedside. Recently my mom passed away, and now she and my dad are celebrating their life together in the presence of Eternal Love.

In the lore of many cultures, the rainbow has been seen as a bridge between heaven and earth, connecting the realm of the spirit with our life in the here and now. This is the way I'd like you to think of the rainbow that is spelled out in this book. The people you'll be meeting in the following pages have bridged the gap between heaven and earth, and have helped bring me closer to God. I share these stories with you in the hope that you also will find in them not just enjoyable reading, but comfort and inspiration.

One

Touched by Red
The Spirit of Love

As a little child, this color became for me a powerful symbol of love, a love that was spontaneous, honest, and genuine, a love that for me needed to be expressed by nothing more than a kind gesture: a red valentine, a red balloon, or even one red rose.

I turned red when I received my first valentine, also red, from someone I admired very much. We were friends in the first grade and are still close friends today.

When I received my first balloon (red, of course), the excitement I felt was so strong that it still comes back to me when I see a similar balloon today. So I decided to bring such a balloon to friends I visited in the hospital and I was pleasantly surprised by the childlike joy on their faces, when I presented them with a balloon. It touched others the same way it touched me.

In my capacity as campus minister, I

made an announcement at all the weekend liturgies about my concern for the sick and lonely in the hospitals and that I was looking for a way to brighten up their lives. I told the students how happy patients were when I brought them a simple colored balloon, and invited them to come to a meeting the following week to discuss a plan of action. Fifty students were interested in the ministry. We set up schedules to visit the hospital on different days, bringing balloons to cancer patients and to children. Though some students had initial doubts about the value of just bringing balloons, they were all pleased that a simple act of giving could bring such joy to the patients.

I was delighted to see how the world blossomed before the students themselves when they saw how easily they could make a real difference in someone's life. I recall one occasion when I was visiting Chris, a friend who was in the hospital. I had brought a student with me, a robust wrestler named Matt. On entering Chris's room, we passed an elderly man in the bed next to him. He looked gaunt and withered from age and loneliness. Immediately on seeing the balloons his eyes sprang to life, thinking they were for him. Nervously, I looked at Matt, then at Chris. Sensing our predicament,

Chris looked at me and smiled. "I understand, you can give them to him," he said.

I handed a bright red balloon to Matt. Walking over to the old man's bed, he held out the balloon. The man's face beamed. It was as if he had just been given his first Christmas present. We were all thrilled to see how happy it made the man. With tears in his eyes the old man smiled and said, "Thank you, thank you. This is the first balloon I ever received. I wanted one all my life, but no one ever gave me one."

Matt asked, "How old are you, old-timer?"

"Ninety."

We were shocked. This man had lived all those years without ever receiving a balloon. Tears of joy filled his eyes, and our eyes too.

"It doesn't take much to make people happy," I thought out loud.

We left the hospital that evening with a warm feeling in our hearts. I wondered who benefited more from our visit, the old man or ourselves.

I could tell by the sparkle in his eyes that the red balloon was an expression of love to him.

The following stories show how love is expressed and lived by people I've met along my journey.

Finding Love and Friendship
Where I Least Expected

In May 1996 I had the wonderful opportunity of visiting mainland China as part of a group led by Dennis Lou, an adviser to the Chinese government on education and trade matters. At first I was reluctant to go because of all the negative press I had been reading about China, and all the bad news on TV, especially since the Tienanmen Square massacre. Frankly, I was frightened, but I decided to go, after reflecting on one of my favorite Bible verses, "Trust in God with all your heart; do not depend on your own understanding. Seek God's will in all you do, and God will direct your paths" (adapted from Proverbs 3:5–6).

When we arrived in China, we could not have been greeted with more genuine affection and courtesy. As the days passed, we came to realize that the political circumstances of the country could in no way cover up the beautiful spirit of the many people I met. Their kindness and attentiveness, the spontaneity of their friendship, put me at ease and made me feel welcome.

The first place we stayed was an advanced

vocational and technical school. The officials and students could not have been more gracious. Their sincere desire to learn all they could about me, about who I was and what I did, made me feel instantly at home. When the students learned that I liked to dance, they pleaded with me to teach them American steps, and arranged to have a dance the following night. Talk about being put on the spot!

Excitement about the presence of visitors and about the dance spread throughout the campus. The next day students and teachers alike approached me to practice their English. Among a thousand different questions, they asked what kind of dances I was going to teach them, where I lived in America, what my family was like, how many brothers and sisters I had. Their excitement was infectious.

When evening came, people began gathering at the dance hall. In no time it was filled. Chinese music was playing softly in the background. The room glowed with soft red lights turned down low. Many of the girls were dressed in red. They were not at all shy about getting out on the dance floor and learning the new steps, thoroughly enjoying the challenge. The boys, just like American boys, were content to sit on the sidelines and girl-watch. It wasn't long, though, before they all caught the spirit, and every boy in the place was dancing. The professors eventually joined in, and even the president of the school took part. The students had never danced with the faculty before, but somehow this night was different. We were just a family of fun-loving young-at-hearts having a good time together. The electric slide seemed to be everybody's favorite. "Now we know some American dances," they cried out happily. The way they danced made obvious their passion for having fun. It brought back memories of my last Easter at Kalamazoo when I had been listening to polka music on my way to church. As I drove into the parking lot and saw the trumpet player waiting for me to open the church, I turned the music up loud and jumped out of the car and said, "Ken, how about celebrating Easter and dancing the polka?" We danced up a storm, laughing so hard that at first we didn't notice my car slowly rolling down the incline toward the street. Fortunately, I caught it just in time. But that didn't stop us from continuing our polka. Totally unaware of anything around us, we didn't notice the pastor driving into the parking lot. Our faces turned red when we realized he was watching. He just shook his head and laughed. "I don't believe you sometimes, Dort."

In the dance hall that night, the Chinese students showed that same childlike joy. Maybe that is why the people I met in China clung to me. They were curious and so many times said to me, "You seem so happy, what is it that brings you such joy? You seem so free, is your family like that too?" They also asked a lot of questions about God. They did not know that I was a nun, which made it all the more surprising. In fact, one afternoon two women interpreters took me shopping. They had been very polite and professional while in business sessions, but now that we were by ourselves and away from their administrators, the ladies in no time at all reverted to being like little girls, laughing and giggling as they encouraged me to try on a bright red kimono. "We love red, even our wedding dresses are red," they told me. The salesladies helping us were delighted to see how much fun we were having. What impressed me the most was the spontaneous warmth and sincerity that flowed from each person I met.

When we visited the University of Shantou, we were given the same warm reception, and became the object of the same curiosity. The people, all so well educated, had the curiosity of little children. Here I was even more impressed with their interest in spirituality. A very bright elderly man who had been the commander of the armies that conquered South China during the revolution expressed a keen interest in spirituality, and said it was something the Chinese people very much needed. This man had also been the mayor of Shantou and built it into the most beautiful and progressive city in the country. He shared his concern about the children's desperate need for role models and spiritual values. The same concern was expressed by Madame Zhu Xi Nan, the director of education for the district of Guilin. The depth of her spirituality came alive after our short encounter.

As I reflect on all my experiences in China, so many thoughts go through my mind: things I saw, things people shared with me, and how these beautiful people touched my life. One for example, still haunts me.

I was horrified by the Chinese government's rigid laws allowing only one child per family. In a conversation one day with a college professor, I asked her bluntly, "Is it really true the government forces you to have abortions?"

"It is the law, but it is enforced only if you are a public official in a prominent position working in Beijing. Otherwise, the government merely fines ordinary citizens for each child after the first one."

She then came back with a remark that startled me. "With all the trouble we have in struggling to keep our children, it is difficult for us to understand why American women are so happy they are allowed to kill their own babies, and we aren't even Christian."

I was too shocked to respond. I wanted to counter what she said, but was lost for words. I've never seen the issue defined so strikingly before. Thinking about it afterward, I became more convinced than ever of the great possibility for spiritual growth that lies in the hearts of the Chinese people.

Although these people have not yet found God, they seem to be yearning for a life that is still beyond their grasp. It broke my heart to feel so helpless in the face of such raw spiritual hunger. I realized I could do nothing to introduce these people to an inner life of the Spirit for which they are starving. It is not rice, fish, or bread the Chinese people crave. It's the spirituality that we in our Western Christian civilization find so easy to lay aside as we bask in material luxury.

My time spent in China made me aware of the needs of my brothers and sisters in faraway places. My experience, so different from all that I read in the papers, has opened my heart to those people, who before were a mystery. Now I know them as people so much like myself, with the same dreams, the same needs, the same struggles to be free from those things that stifle the spirit.

Happily, my relationship with Madame Zhu did not end in China. The following February she was invited by the United States Congress to come to the National Prayer Breakfast in Washington. She was deeply impressed being part of four thousand people praying for one another and for peace in the world. Afterward she came to Joshua to spend time with me. We had a delightful few days. We shared memories of the past and dreams of the future, and stomped through the deep snow like two teenage girls.

When I drove her to the airport to catch her flight home, she said to me, "There are three people who live at Joshua."

"No," I said, "there are only two."

"No," she insisted, "there are three. You, Father Joe, and God. I know, because I felt God's presence there. I know God is there."

I was deeply touched that this gentle, brilliant woman, who did not know of God before, should reveal so much of the richness of her own inner life in so few words.

Her remark brought tears to my eyes. It was such a joy to hear that this gentle, brilliant woman had felt God's presence in our home. It also showed the depth and clarity of her mind that she could reveal so much of herself in so few words.

That this woman, who had previously felt that she did not know God at all should suddenly be shown God's great presence and mercy is amazing to me.

When she left the gate for the plane she could not look back. I am sure she felt the same pain in her heart that I felt in mine. Spirituality comes alive when we know we are loved and accepted for who we are. It was obvious she felt accepted and loved.

People are placed in our life to help us see that God's goodness is very much alive even where we least expect it. My heart has been touched and colored by the love I received while in China. My experience there was, and continues to be, like a living valentine.

Love — Ever Faithful

When we think of fidelity, we think of it in its ideal form, without blemish, a fidelity that never falters, a fidelity that is like cold steel. Unfortunately, we will never find this ideal in human flesh. Human virtues are the result of lifelong efforts toward an ideal, not the result of instantaneous grace. At the end of life we may have arrived at a certain superior level of faithfulness, but even then we will fall far short of the divine ideal. Human faithfulness should more properly be measured by our tenacity to stay focused on a commitment, whether it be to a person, an ideal, or a cause, no matter how many times we may fall. As humans, we have to expect to fall and stumble along the way. Even Moses, David, and Peter failed God after he placed so much trust in them. What is beautiful in them is their rising up after falling, even falling miserably, and continuing the struggle to be faithful.

It was snowing the day Carrie and Ben were married, but still the whole town showed up to share their joy. They were a lighthearted, happy couple. Everyone knew they were the perfect match.

For years their marriage was an endless

romance. They had so many things in common that it was rare when they were not doing something together. As they were raised in different religious traditions, they decided not to let the Church come between them, so religion was not a part of their life.

As time went on, Carrie grew restless. Something was missing. She still loved Ben immensely and loved being with him, but something was happening at work of which she was totally unaware. Aaron, a fellow employee, started meeting Carrie for lunch, which was quite normal since the employees all went out to lunch together. Gradually, however, subtle changes in Carrie's feelings were taking place. For a while they passed unnoticed. But when she started to find herself getting depressed when Aaron did not show up for lunch, she knew something was happening to her. She was falling in love with him. She panicked. She missed him and felt miserable when they were apart.

At home Ben noticed a change in her but could not understand it. Even though they still enjoyed doing things together, Carrie seemed aloof and irritable, snapping at Ben for the simplest things. When he would ask what was the matter, all she would do was cry. She had always been open and honest